To Love a Dandelion.

Lauren Williamson

Copyright © 2023
Lauren Williamson

For the Weeds.

Table of Contents

With Wolves - 9
Yarrow - 11
In Lavendula's Lace - 13
Sanctum - 15
Aseptic - 17
Initiation - 19
Crone - 21
Extant - 23
Muse of A Lifetime - 25
The Times - 27
Anima - 29
Wallflower - 31
Mute - 33
Meet - 35
Birdbrain - 37
Purloined - 39
Phoenix - 41
Hush - 43
In Mirrors - 45
Flesh & Bone - 47
Noxious - 49
Love, Love Not - 51
Burst - 53
Songbird - 55

Salt & Sand - 57
Memory – 59
Marigold - 61
Sovereign - 63
Carrion - 65
The Monarchs - 67
Home - 69
Lions - 71
Wayward - 73
Witching - 75
12am - 77
Gasp - 79
Dogma - 81
Vicarious - 83
Roses - 85
The Knowing of Grey - 87
In Willows - 89
To the Bees - 91
Phantoms - 93
Red - 95
Sinew - 97
Sleepless - 99
Seaside - 101
In Thick – 103
The Hollowing - 105
For the Dreamers - 107

Starseed - 109
Dark Horse - 111
Caw - 113
Wilting Green - 115
In Stone - 117
Rings - 119
Aerie - 121
Weep - 123
Lineage - 125
Tempest - 127
Untethered - 129
Lions & Lovers - 131
Magnolia - 133
In Three - 135
Recycle - 137
Intuition - 139
Fawn - 141
For the Art - 143
To Love a Dandelion - 145

Dip me in slow words.
I want the ones
That honey sticks to,
The kind that amble
And hold on tight.
Dust me in old days.
I'm sweet for the way vintage
Postures and poses
On contemporary skin.
Lose me in the witching hours.
The waning microcosm
Where soapbox voices
Bleach into inky night.
Drop me in the wild.
Where the wolves
Roam and wail,
Lulling this season softly,
Into the mayhem of mind.

- With Wolves

One thousand ways to mend.
Show me the land
Where the yarrow lives.
Where snow white petals
Will water ashes.
I cannot believe this place,
Not until you show me
And the throes of Spring
Take us whole
And we remember ourselves
As sentient
And creatures of virtue.
You say there are
One thousand ways,
I am asking only,
For one.

- Yarrow

See to it she knows,
What is hush
Breathes through lace lungs
And raw is the heart,
Whose secrets are bare
And whose threads of filigree
Dance in the silk
Of necrotic night scape.

- In Lavandula's Lace

In the thickest trees
I do not go
To be seen by the world,
Acknowledged or held.
I go simply to be gazed at
By forest eyes,
To be breathed in
By the tall ones.
To know,
I am small among them,
But mighty
And of their wild.

- Sanctum

Lie to me,
And in the lark I'll join.
To withered notion
I'll play changeling,
And smear hand prints
Across all you've cleaned.

- Aseptic

Today is risk.
Drained,
The delicate hands
Of youth's embrace.
Today is unkempt
And initiation.
Today is the wild.

- Initiation

Foot of crow stalk,
The walking of the birds
Birthing sentries of sagacity
That lurk in crevice.
And silver strands
Rope through
What is bramble
But sometimes silk.
Traded porcelain
For lines that breathe
And move with no bother of time,
No regard for the dents of vanity
But a grace,
A glory
For lived in skin
And bones with a back.
For deliverance
And immunity
From the plight
Of what is skittish
And sullen,
Callow,
Broken and kept.

Oh, one that has roamed
Raw Earth,
Torrid skies
And wicked seas,
You are cunning breath
And new life.

- Crone

When I walk through the forests,
The ones with the ferns,
There is magic.
The ferns, ancient.
Unchanged from primeval inception.
In the forests with the ferns,
I hear them whisper,
"Leave us,
We know how to survive."

- Extant

As a muse she was exceptional.
A work in constant progress.
Because time is slow,
And always arriving.

- Muse of a Lifetime

I've purposely tipped the glass
And the edge runs.
Ink in water,
Dancing and drowning,
Fluidity crowning black pools
Into a smudge of absolution.
And I cave and carve paper wings
From newsprint running
Old stories,
Calling for a revival
A coming of age.
But instead
Fawning and complicit,
And drawing days backwards,
Into ink that is settled,
And feature stories,
That read left to right.

- The Times

Hollow dance,
Steal anima
And leave pale lace
Across skin that crawls
On tiny Bluebells.
Can you see them now?
Embroidered but barely
Against threadbare cotton
One hundred years young.
Can you taste my fixation
On flora that cannot bloom
And fauna dulled and dilute?
In this idle garden
You are water
And I am fire,
Opposite marrow
In inverse bone.
Oh blasphemous
Dance of decay,
We can know love
By one hundred names
But this waltz,
Is not one.

- Anima

Weary are bones
Of fading ruse,
Of disciples on display
Taming feral seek.
Maybe this enduring,
Is unveiling.

- Wallflower

They're just elegant characters.
Shapes we've come to taste
And fasten together
To give nuance
To the wordless
That combusts within.
But they don't always get it right.
Sometimes the deepest
And dismal
And most abstruse
Go without elegant characters
Because there is no elegance.
What exactly,
Do we do with those?

- Mute

Trace the longing and lust
That keeps you up until the edge
Where night crashes into day.
And take me to the place
Where the breath of the world
Enters your toes
And has its way with the flesh
That craves in between.
Show me what stays
And what leaves
When you sip
The sound of winter
And taste the cold
That bites your bones.
Work your way backwards
From now
And into the memoirs
Of then and yesterday.
Don't skip a single part
That stirs what has bruised
Or built you.
Tell me the things
You have kept over the years,

The ones that have fashioned you
And bound you
And broke you.
Show me the scars
And unpack the healing, or not
From start to finish.
And from this place,
When you weep,
Smile,
Laugh,
Or bleed,
I will see you as one,
I will know you,
As whole.

- Meet

From the view of the birds
We are flame
And flood
Flailing
And falling.
Willfully following
But instead drowning
With filth on shoulders
And mud in mind.
From sky down,
We are busy
But not like the bees
And not like the ants
We are one for one
And all for none.
From the view of the birds
The winged ones frown,
Hum somber songs
And fly away.

- Birdbrain

Give back the words.
On all the days
There are crooks that rob
And gouge
And pillage
Prose from lips
And rhythm from soul.
Oh heartache,
Bellow your songs.
Your notes are faint
And familiar
But flat
And sharp
And missing the verses
That birth dance
And the choruses
Of life
And lust,
The ones we used to know.
We are dull
And melody starved.
Watered down
And edgeless.

- Purloined

We rose from ashes,
Time and time again.
Because burning down
Was beautiful
And part of the story.
From ashes,
We wrote prose
On typewriters
As dated as we were.

- Phoenix

Tell me you see the irony
In the way we move
And the way time stalks.
We are slow
And methodically
Tying ourselves to legacy
And how it lives
And where it goes
When the dark calls
And our names slip beneath.
Hush.
We are made,
Only of mist.

- Hush

In mirrors,
We are calling back reflections.
Days we have survived.
Breath we have expired.
History we have abandoned.
And a thousand minutes walk
Between those and these.
In mirrors,
Lives total absence
Of presence.

- In Mirrors

Do not call us sheep
But watch us graze
On poison pastures
We have not sown,
Have not tended,
Have not chosen.
Do not sheer
What lives on skin
But bear witness
To unhinged blood
In cunning flock bones.
Do not call in the dogs
To herd, tame
Or tuck us away.
We are wild and content,
Running deviant lines,
With flesh starved wolves.

- Flesh & Bone

We've put it all on them.

They weep.

Harder than we do.

For what was.

What has come.

What has gone.

There is nothing here.

Only weakened soil

To root feet.

And poison skies

To stretch limbs.

They breathe,

Exchanging,

The things we've done.

- Noxious

These fields have held us.
For ages,
For lifetimes.
As we pick alternating petals
From daisy stems,
With botanical certainty,
I know,
Love ghosts live here.

- Love, Love Not

Seed in ground,
Wail.
What lies above is barren,
There is no seduction.
No legacy.
No praise for your ancient art,
For the burrow,
For the burst,
For the wild bloom.
Seed in ground,
Wait.
Nestled in the asylum
Of the ancestors,
Of sacred stone,
Of earth and clay.
It's sullen gospel,
What is above
Is not as below.

Seed in ground,

Here,

Where the sun cremates

And the septic winds dance

There is only wasteland

And fruitless vow,

Of monstrous decay.

- Burst

A fallen bird
Lay outside my door today.
His earthly decent pillowed
By January's snow.
In days gone,
I must have
Heard him voice
Two hundred hymns
From the Pines above.
Watched him flutter
Between Spruce branches
And dance wild and free
In and out of the Maples.
Oh, what a remarkable life
This sweet one has lived.
What an enduring gift it is,
To have known his song.

- Songbird

Letters to the sea,
I write in salt and sand
And lose words in the mist
And reminisce on
Vanishing time
And space that was costly
And shallow.
To you I gave mine,
Brazen in the taking.
We have played
Through seasons
And song.
In this apathy
We are in,
And out with the tide.

- Salt & Sand

Like chords from then,
You play on broken strings.
I sing the softest haunting.
And you forget the words.
This orchestra
Is brilliance
And breaking
And I give my memory
Where yours has gone.
Time has lapsed
And into what waits,
Together we will fall.

- Memory

Lie flat in marigold fields
Where we can mute
Our most curated selves.
Where we can sink
Beneath the weight
Of floral froth,
Damned by the vices
Of worldly affairs.
Lie flat in marigold fields,
Where when they call,
We can tuck away
And plant our bodies.
In dark and day.
We are untouched,
Living among
The marigolds.

- Marigold

This crown has no jewels.
There are no false riches
In this crown.
Seize the vices
That cage her wild.
This crown
Is daisies and freedom.

- Sovereign

Autumn left ghosts.
In outlines,
The vanity of
Summer sulked
With petals
And colors
And green
On the ground.
Out of nowhere,
You said,
Goodwill was lost.
And without words
And in muted ways,
I stared down
At metaphors.
In Autumn's carrion,
You have named
The feral weeds within.

- Carrion

Where the monarchs flew
There is drought.
No air moves,
No water flows.
What has been built
Is baroque and perilous,
Lucid, yet bred from bad dreams.
And I climb stairs
To pull away
But vertigo leaves me tumbling
And breaking queasy knees.
I am tangled and wordless.
Without liberation in sight,
I keep only what's been left.
This is life,
On patterned wings.

- The Monarchs

This land will call you in.
And in the darkest grey
Through the wind
That eats holes in bones,
This land will know what you are.
And the floral summon of Spring
Will bite early
And bear the weight
Of one hundred rains.
And you will fall,
Beneath the canopy
Of the oldest wood
And the heaviest veil.
This land will teach you earth
And draw you in
To the savior of the sea.
And from the gardens
You have turned,
This land will pluck thorns
And dress you up and down

In salt water hunger
And mud puddle stains.
In dew covered days
You are seedling
And this land,
Will grow you a home.

- Home

This house so empty,
A carnival of lost cause.
We tiptoe lightly
To not stir what lies in wait.
We are not searching
For the place hope lives.
We are basking
In all we've moved from.
In countless ways,
This feels like feeding
The lions we have survived.

- Lions

Something stirs here.
I don't have a finger
To put on it.
But there is wild,
It lives
On your breath.
And in this I know,
You are both,
Ravenous
And starving love.

- Wayward

Stray with me
Into the dark hours,
Where the offspring
Of stillness and silence play.
Do not leave the light on,
Just loosen.
Slip beneath
Into coal cloaked thresholds
Where night chokes day
In a lethargic
And calculated
Culling of illumination.
Dip into the world
Where hibernation lives
But bounty awaits the hunger
Of the after hours hunter.
Nest deep,
Here in the woods
Of the insomnious,
Where the fruitless mind
Is parched but pliable,
And fit without flaw to unearth
The delicacies of darkness.

With eyes wide open,
Let the sweet refuge of light
Fail and fold us.
This is the land of shadows,
And we have come.

- Witching

These mornings remember,
The ways you
Crept through dreams
And tangled in hours
Not meant for you.
Between sheets you lie dormant
And I can leave you behind.
In midnight illusion,
You are the safest.

- 12am

Glass,
The forest floor
Breathes beneath.
Do not dance and do not tap.
There is no way through.
No darkness to bury toes
Or seeds,
Or secrets,
This land is fragile.
Lie flat on the crystal earth,
Place lips on sealed mud,
And step away clean.
Poke fingers at the creatures,
There are no creatures,
What is encased
Is sterile and barren.
We do not put our hopes
For Spring's sweet renewal
Or Summer's lust and bloom
In this forsaken terrain anymore.
In these withered acres,
There is no song,
The birds do not sing,

In revolt of insolence,
There is only
The righteous temper
Of fire, water, earth and air
Come children,
Look, see,
Beneath the glass,
The forest floor
Barely breathes.

- Gasp

Our bodies are haunted.
Prey of gospel,
We are live-in ghosts
That dance and blow
And in docile doctrine
Plant flawed hearts
In bitter blackish places
Where on purpose,
No saintly dawn
Or day will brush.
Where the mass
Of what freezes
Will snap specter bones
And polar breath will poison
And savor the succulence of
What's still human.
And we'll ask,
Through a post-coital blur of
Sunday worship and seance,
"What exactly,
Is still human?"

- Dogma

In mine I hold
The hands of a stranger.
And there is blight
And bright
And rehearsed alive.
In lines there are stories
And secrets,
Like thieves are thick.
And there are scars
That scold maiden skin
And a scholar's touch.
In mine I have lived,
Through the hands
Of a stranger.

- Vicarious

Here are the secrets we keep,
Buried beneath the roses.
Pruned and trimmed,
We are coral and yellow
And living in color.
But we know too well,
The crimson wilt.
In the roses,
Our skeletons grow.

- Roses

Seize in greyscale
The monochromatic tones of day.
And stay just long enough
To trace lines on foreheads
Into pinpoint wisdom.
And from this sketch,
Learn to live in air with the sages.
Oh, what offering to bring?
With or without
The sacrifice of gold.
And where in silver timelines,
Come and gone,
Do we peel to nude
And stop brushing over
All that has left us longing for hue?
These crowded dimensions
Have drawn shadow shades.
We are pleading for color
And knowing,
Only the greyest parts.

- The Knowing of Grey

The willows are
Breaking,
Bending
And binding
But as beasts,
We tear at embrace,
Imprisoned by what
Will surely save us.
The willows are victory
And we are simple fear,
Bathed in whispy limbs.

- In Willows

The bees are bitter.
Can you blame them?
From groves we've plucked
Sustenance to place
Dead and dying
In the center
Of round kitchen tables,
With deep desires
To lighten moods
And offer contrast
To the exhausted means
By which we converse
From throats
And rarely from hearts.
We ask so much
And give so little.

- To the Bees

In the wind we tangle
And phantoms
Move through body
And echo through mind.
This place,
Has nothing to do
With the blood
That runs through
Human veins.

- Phantoms

Bring something red.
Something that breathes
The days you have been.
Bring something
That has warmed bones
In the February wild.
Something exposed
And naked,
Crude
And ancient.
Leave it behind
If it fits in bare hands
Or in the matter that is mind.
Bring here only,
Something that has lived.

- Red

Loot from queen
And pitch a masquerade.
This cage of bones is laid bare
And weaving rival sinew.
In this porcelain parade
Charcoal theory has longed,
For a wisdom in wildfire
And the art of burning down.
And with rebirth,
Stare into the novas
And past the virgin prose.
And witness the givers,
Of sense and self
And storm and song.
Oh duality,
Eyes to the sky,
Sing, sing, sing
All that's been cloying.
We are wolf in fog
And we are battle born.

- Sincw

In the placid hours,
Where the black sheep dance
Through fable and allegory
There is only sustenance,
A feeding of the unmet.
And in this barren hunt,
Where limbs lock
And veins frey
The refuge of home,
Perilously howls,
We are not the same.

- Sleepless

When I am by the sea,
The backside world stops.
If only for this time,
We part ways
And I have grown
As a limb of something else.
There is only this novel existence
And the way it moves,
The way it calls one into play.
And though feet on earth,
I have devotedly become
A step in its dance,
A note in its hymn,
A drop in its ancestry.
Just one drop
And that is perfectly enough.

- Seaside

It was in those minutes.
Those moments
When it was all falling.
We realized,
We belonged
To all the beautiful stories,
Just past this place.

- In Thick

In what way precisely
Does the howling
Blow through?
Does it birth at toes
And rove past knees
Or does it weep
From ether
And wail sweet nothings,
Hailing in hooking tones?
And tell me,
By the time it
Ebbs through chambers
And flows into the
Belly of skin and soul
What parts and pieces
And tokens and trinkets
Has the howling stalked
And poached as its own?
What truly does it spare
Of an essence blotted out
And when it leaves,
Does it ever really go?

- The Howling

Nobody dreams here.
We are wrapped,
Engulfed,
Entrenched,
And chewing pieces
That are awkward
And angular.
Here, there is no shelter
For the dreamers.

- For the Dreamers

She belonged to time,
And to the stars
And the seeds
And the wild in our bones.
She sung her sweetest melody
And something in us healed.
She belonged to the infinite.
And inside of souls,
Her symphony bloomed.

- Star Seed

Dark horse,
Write us your tale of origin.
Pull us through the aftermath
Where you mime your softest self.
Lucid we are to the charlatan
You keep us from.
In your eyes we know,
You are the truest.

- Dark Horse

I am sometimes
Made of eggshells
And sometimes
Wail and pull
On the song of the crows.
Bold, bold, bold.
But also brittle,
And in the throes
Of riotous confession,
Rough,
Woven,
Then spun to silk.
In the space between lips
I am cerebral and pallid
A complexion for complexity.
I am searching
For bird words,
Ravenous for something
Not there.

- Caw

At the edge of this garden,
Our softest stories are wilting.
We are not tending,
Growing,
Blooming.
At the edge of this garden,
Our greenest selves
Are showing.

- Wilting Green

Paint us on walls
With hips that bear,
Toes that cradle the earth
And arms that run to the veil.
Draw the iron
That moves through blood
And pumps through
Parts not of them.
And in the creators,
Know the weight
Of what is birthed
And the bed it grows.
From lines,
We are speaking lineage.
From clay,
We are showing you
Ancient stone.

- In Stone

Sever this twine,
Binding leaf to branch.
We are the keepers
Of lingering seasons,
Far past their prime.
Where night soil claims fog
Our silver minds hover in wait,
Leave us to roam here.
We are not
The ignorance of January
Or faculties of youth
But molted skins,
And inner rings.
Groundless and wild.

- Rings

Wayfarer amble,
Through the turn of months
And seasons that mutate.
Dormant we wait
For backbones to rebuild
And spines to straighten
And strengthen.
And we lust,
Sparrows of the wild
For the wind
We call home
And the songs we savor
In nests that are hollow
And iron cages,
Mostly bitter,
Seldom sweet.
What has fluttered
And lived
And loved
Has long past or flown.
We are vagabond wings,
With no sovereign air to fly.

- Aerie

Willow can you lose me?
Can you tie me into your limbs,
And pull me into weathered skin?
I long to weep with
No remorse,
Like you Willow.
Weep for the myth of perpetuation,
Weep for the veil,
Weep for the ones we have been.
Can you weave me Willow?
Can you take split threads,
And teach them to tumble wild
Through wind, rain and storm?
I have yearned for the other side
Of this woe.
But Willow,
You have learned instead
To lament and to live,
To love and to lose,
To blow fierce,
Through bitter land
And back again.

- Weep

As the world
Bellowed out for more,
We climbed up and out.
And with the sweetest
Taste of ascent,
We understood,
We are not all we inherit.

- Lineage

Come close and tell me now,
Are you afraid of the night
And what lives in the storm?
If so, I'll go my way
And you go yours.

- Tempest

Good Mother let go.
Let rudimentary dreams
And half-lived flesh and blood
Fall, fall, fall
From the safest hearth
And the asylum of heart.
In pockets we keep
The wisdom of lineage
And in bones you live
But Good Mother
Cut them loose.
Shove them to initiation,
Into land that is foreign
For the world to bite,
Teething at ankles
And untethering soul.
Good Mother
They have been yours to hold
But being of the wild,
Is their name.

- Untethered

Tell me about the
Lions and the lovers.
Tell me of the ones
You have torn
And the ones
That have left you open.
Show me the ways
They have laid thorns
And then walk me back
On their silk
And softness.
Spare me nothing,
When you speak of
The lions and the lovers
And in the dusk
Before day breaks,
I will know our game.

- Lions & Lovers

Burst magnolia from boreal days
And breathe sweet mercy into a frost
That has built frail bones.
In sun and withered seasons
Come and gone,
Draw vigor from
Bruised and torn buds.
Feed flame Magnolia,
And from the claws of crooks
Salvage what is yours.
Torch to tinder,
Dragon fire is of you.

- Magnolia

In gifts of verse,
Short and to the point,
Burn what you have built
And show us the power of three.
Make us believe,
In the song of your voice
And the wind,
Of revolution.

- In Three

When I write,

In this bleakest of era,

The paper starves.

Hungry teeth snarl,

And I weep for the trees

As I waste their skin

With poorly constructed prose

And words that don't belong.

- Recycle

The winds and the birds
Are better fortune tellers
Of cobalt blue minds
And aversion
Then most.
On days like these ones,
I go where they go.
It's a hunch.

- Intuition

Behind glass we live.
Away from the ivy that creeps
And steals the fawn
To the impurity of dreams.
Who riddles the way
And walks the Doe,
From a memory of stone
To a lifeless forest
Of teething giants
And keepers of sin.
In the panic of night
And from the cries
Of what lives
Between dark and dawn,
We know your origin
And we have learned
To run to the hills.
With panes
We have placed land,
Between the timber
You have burned
And the saplings
We have grown.

- Fawn

Come to the water
Where the edges melt
And the fancy crows play.
There is drought
And bones
And bits
Of the crumbs
We left to the birds.
Come to the water,
To the cathedral of art
And gesture the grand undoing.
This edge is a guild of mania.

- For the Art

Not weeds.
We are labelers,
Crafters of crates
And thirsty to crush
What lives between here
And manicured utopias.
But this ornamental prestige,
It's bland on lips
And rarely satiates
The longing, the lust
For thorns that bloom wild.
In this life,
I will love the dandelions,
Like the flowers they are.

- To Love A Dandelion